WORLD'S WEIRDEST
BUGS
AND OTHER CREEPY CREATURES

by M.L. Roberts

*Consultant: Dr. Norman I. Platnick, Chairman and Curator,
Department of Entomology, American Museum of Natural History*

Troll Associates

DON'T PINCH ME!

THE HERCULES BEETLE

Imagine walking around with a big pair of pliers on your head! That's pretty much what male Hercules beetles do. A pair of hornlike pincers opens and closes whenever the beetle moves his head.

There are about 300,000 different types of beetles in the world, and the Hercules beetle is one of the largest. A male can measure up to 7 inches (18 cm) long from the tip of the horns to the end of the abdomen. Because females don't have horns on their heads, they are much smaller.

You might say a beetle's body is inside out. That's because its skeleton is on the *outside*! This tough *exoskeleton* is like a suit of armor, and it protects the beetle from danger.

THE BIG STING

THE GIANT HORNET

This insect should have a "Do Not Disturb" sign on its nest! Hornets usually build their nests in trees and bushes, and they definitely *don't* want anyone to touch them. If a person or an animal comes too close, the hornets will swarm out and sting the intruder again and again.

Hornets are members of the wasp family. Their nests are made of paper. The queen hornet starts the nest by chewing up wood and plants and turning the material into a kind of paper. As more hornets are born, they all help make the nest bigger.

Hornets may have a nasty sting, but they also help people by eating flies, caterpillars, and other pests. So the hornet is your friend — as long as you keep your distance!

Like many insects, hornets have two types of eyes. Two big *compound eyes* sit one on each side of its head. In between the compound eyes are three simple eyes or *ocelli.* These smaller eyes are probably used to sense light and darkness, while the compound eyes give the hornet a true picture of the world. Talk about seeing double!

SAY YOUR PRAYERS

THE PRAYING MANTIS

This large insect may look like it's praying. But other insects who come too close are the ones who'd better say their prayers! A mantis has strong forelegs that open and close like the blade of a pocketknife. When another insect comes too close — zap! The mantis grabs its prey and shoves it in its mouth. It usually doesn't even bother to kill its dinner before it starts to eat!

Praying mantises are so fierce, it's hard for them to mate. Because the female is likely to attack anything that comes near her, the male must approach very slowly. Otherwise, she'll bite his head off, and the wedding will turn into a funeral!

Believe it or not, praying mantises can make good pets. They kill flies and other insect pests, and will even eat out of your hand. You can even "pet" it — the mantis seems to enjoy having its back stroked!

A STICKY SITUATION

THE GARDEN SPIDER

What has 8 legs, 8 eyes (usually), spins silk — and is *not* an insect? A spider! Spiders are members of the arachnid group. While insects have 6 legs and a body that is made up of 3 parts, spiders have 8 legs and a 2-part body. Also, insects often have wings or antennae, but an arachnid never does.

The garden spider uses its web to catch its dinner. The spider hangs in the middle of its web, waiting for an insect to fly too close and get caught in the sticky strands. When the spider feels movement in its web, it rushes out to investigate. It wraps its prey up with more sticky silk threads, then bites the insect with its fangs to inject a poison that kills or paralyzes it. If the spider is hungry, it will eat its dinner right away. If not, it might hang the insect in its web and save it for a snack later on.

The arachnids get their name from an old Greek myth. Once upon a time, there was a girl named Arachne who was the best weaver in her village. She challenged the goddess Athena to a weaving contest. Athena was so jealous of Arachne's skill that she turned the girl into a spider. What a sore loser!

ROW, ROW, ROW
YOUR BOAT

THE GIANT WATER BUG

Giant water bugs are also called toe biters or electric light bugs. They have long, flattened back legs, which they use like oars. These bugs "row" through the water or dive to the bottom. They use their front legs to catch insects and tadpoles for food.

The male giant water bug in this picture is carrying eggs on its back. Many insects lay their eggs individually. Others lay a large egg container which is filled with many small eggs.

How can an insect breathe underwater? There are several different ways. Some come to the surface and collect air bubbles under their wings or body and carry them under the water when they dive. They breathe from the air bubbles through openings on the abdomen called *spiracles*. Some use gills to take oxygen from the water, much like a fish. And others have a dense coat of hair on the body which traps air and extracts oxygen from the water.

WHAT BIG EYES YOU HAVE!

THE HORSEFLY

Have you ever tried to swat a fly, only to have it zip away at the last second? The truth is, it's very hard to sneak up on a fly. That's because the fly has a huge compound eye on each side of its head. Each eye is made up of thousands of smaller eyes. So no matter what direction you're approaching from, the fly will always see you coming!

There are many different kinds of flies. Some help us by eating dead animals and other decaying matter. But many flies are terrible pests. They spread disease, destroy crops, spoil food, and bite animals and people. There's no escaping these little creatures, though. Flies are found all over the world — even on the ocean surface near Antarctica!

The wild arum is a plant that relies on flies to pollinate. This plant has a rotten smell that attracts flies. When the flies crawl inside the flower, they are trapped by a ring of guard hairs. As the flies crawl around, pollen sticks to their bodies. The next day, the guard hairs wither and the flies escape. If the flies land on another arum plant, the pollen on their bodies will fertilize its flowers. Now *there's* a plant and an insect that are made for each other!

THE VAMPIRE INSECT

THE LEAFHOPPER

The leafhopper doesn't actually suck its victim's blood like the legendary vampire, but it comes close! This insect's mouth is specially designed for piercing and sucking. It sticks its mouth parts into plants and sucks out the juices inside. Too much of this, and the plant withers and dies. Leafhoppers can also hurt a plant by transmitting fungus or disease.

There are about 15,000 species of leafhoppers. Some, like the one in this picture, are brightly colored. Others are dull green or brown. And leafhoppers aren't very big. They usually measure just $\frac{1}{20}$ to $\frac{3}{4}$ inch (1.3 to 19 mm) long.

Leafhoppers don't have any trouble getting around. They can hop (as you may have guessed from their name), and most species can fly. Leafhoppers are also good runners. But it might be confusing for leafhoppers to have a race — these insects run sideways!

THE LONG AND SHORT OF IT

THE CICADA

You could say cicadas live a long time. Or you could say they're only around for a few weeks. Either way you'd be right!

Cicada young, or *larvae*, live underground and suck juices from tree roots. Some cicadas stay underground for up to 17 years! When they finally become adults, they emerge from the ground and climb trees. All they want to do now is mate and lay eggs. Once that happens, the cicadas die, even though they've been above the ground for only a few weeks!

Cicadas often appear in big groups. You might see them sitting on trees or crawling along the ground. So watch where you step — you wouldn't want to make the adult cicada's life any shorter than it already is!

Cicadas may not be above ground for a long time, but they do make their presence known. A male cicada's abdomen has 2 drumlike sound chambers that make a loud buzzing sound. You may often hear the cicadas' call on a hot summer day.

PHEW!

THE STINK BUG

The stink bug is very well named. When it is threatened, this bug squirts a foul-smelling liquid from large scent glands on the underside of its body. Any creature that was thinking of attacking will run away fast when it gets a whiff of this bug's nasty smell!

Stink bugs eat many different things. Some feed only on insects, while others prefer to eat plants. Many of the stink bugs that feed on plants are green. This makes it hard for other animals to see them, and helps the stink bug eat its meals in peace.

A bad smell isn't the only defense stink bugs have against their enemies. Some scare predators away by the way they look. The stink bug in this picture seems to have eyes sticking out from its head and a row of sharp teeth along the side of its body. But these eyes and teeth are fakes! Most predators won't take any chances, though, and will leave the stink bug alone.

FOLLOW THAT LEAF!

THE LEAF INSECT

Is it a leaf or is it an insect? It's hard to tell with the leaf insect. This creature is usually green, and its wings are shaped just like leaves. It's easy to see how it got its name!

During the day, the leaf insect sits very still on a tree or shrub, perfectly hidden from animals that might want to eat it. At night, the insect feeds on the leaves around it.

A leaf insect's body isn't the only thing that matches its background. Its eggs look just like the seeds of plants. So from birth to death, this is one insect that really becomes part of the scenery!

Leaf insects are related to other insects called walking sticks. These insects look just like twigs. When walking sticks hatch in the spring, they are green to match the new leaves. As they grow older, the insects turn brown — the color of the branches they sit on. What a perfect hiding place!

QUICK-CHANGE ARTIST

THE SPINY OAK SLUG CATERPILLAR

Caterpillars are the magicians of the animal world. Who would ever guess that this wriggly, crawling creature could ever turn into a graceful butterfly or moth?

The main purpose of a caterpillar's life is to eat. After it has stuffed itself with leaves, the caterpillar attaches itself to a twig and changes into a *chrysalis*. Inside the chrysalis, great changes are taking place. The caterpillar's body breaks down into liquid and reforms. It takes weeks — sometimes months — but eventually the chrysalis splits open. Where has the caterpillar gone? It has been transformed into a butterfly or a moth. What a neat trick!

The caterpillar in this picture is quite an eye catcher! Insects that are brightly colored are usually poisonous or bad-tasting. Their colorful bodies warn birds and other predators to stay away. No second helpings, please!

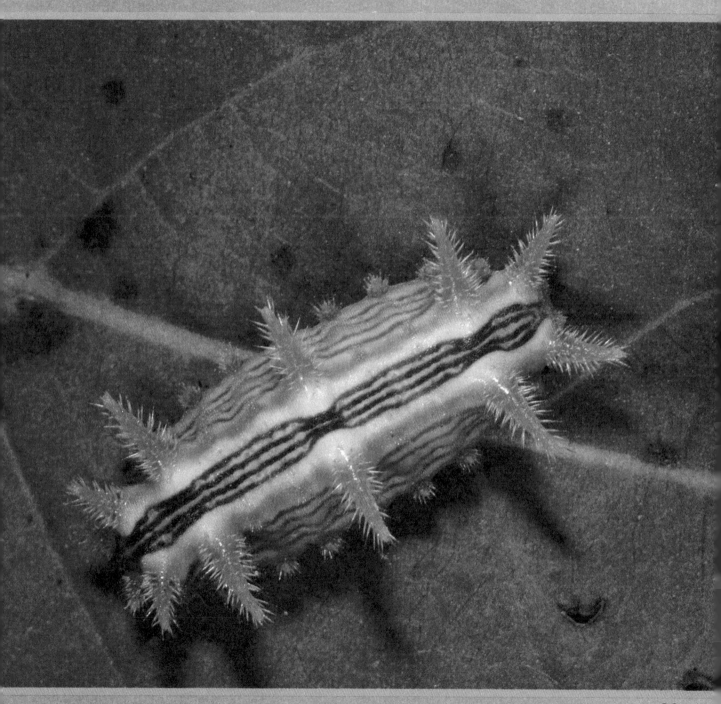

LOOK OUT BELOW!

THE JUMPING SPIDER

Did you know that not all spiders build webs? Instead of quietly waiting for dinner to come along, the jumping spider goes out and hunts it down. This spider has very good eyesight. When it sees an insect it wants to eat, the spider leaps down and injects its prey with a deadly poison. Then it's snack time!

Most jumping animals, such as grasshoppers, rabbits, and kangaroos, have long back legs. But a jumping spider's back legs aren't that much bigger than its other three pairs of legs. But those back legs are strong. In fact, a jumping spider can leap up to 40 times its own length. Someone should enter this fellow in the Animal Olympics!

Jumping spiders may be great leapers, but what happens if they miss? Don't worry — this spider is prepared for anything! It spins a thin length of silk behind it as it jumps. That way, if it misses its target, the silk dragline will save the spider from a bad fall.

JUST SKATING ALONG

THE WATER STRIDER

How would you like to be able to walk on water? The water strider does just that! This insect uses its long legs to skate along the top of the water. Its body never gets wet! The water strider can even jump into the air and land on the water without sinking.

If most insects fall into the water, they will drown. But not the water strider. It feeds on insects trapped in the water by holding its prey with its short front legs.

Most types of water striders live in ponds or streams. But one type, the Pacific water strider, lives on the ocean! Do you think it likes to surf on the big ocean waves?

A GOURMET TREAT?

THE DUNG SCARAB BEETLE

It's a dirty job, but somebody has to do it. The dung beetle feeds on dung, or animal droppings. These beetles roll the dung into a ball and push it into a hole in the ground. Then the beetles crawl in after it to have their dinner. The adult deposits an egg, and the larva develops in the burrow.

That spiky horn on the dung beetle's head isn't just for decoration. It's a weapon! Usually only the male beetles have large horns. They use them in fights with other beetles. The horn is handy for flipping another beetle onto its back, or knocking it into the air.

You might think a beetle is just a beetle, but to the ancient Egyptians, it was an important symbol! Beetles called scarabs were a symbol of life after death. The Egyptians used scarab designs in jewelry and paintings.

SINGING SUPERSTAR

THE MOTTLED SAND GRASSHOPPER

Lots of insects make noise, but the grasshopper makes music! Males "sing" by rubbing their legs and wings together. A row of knobs on the back legs makes the wings vibrate. The male of each type of grasshopper sings a different song, so only females of the same species are attracted to the sound.

Grasshopper legs are good for more than making music. They also make the grasshopper a long jumper! If you startle a grasshopper, it will push off with its strong back legs and leap into the air. Grasshoppers have wings, but they rarely fly. Instead, the wings help the grasshopper glide farther when it jumps.

Some types of grasshoppers can be very destructive. At one time, huge swarms of them sometimes swept down on a field and ate every plant in sight. Entire crops could be wiped out. Today, pesticides help control grasshoppers and prevent such widespread damage.

Index

Page numbers in **bold** indicate photograph.

LIBRARY OF CONGRESS CATALOGING-IN-PUBLICATION DATA
Roberts, M.L. (date)
    World's weirdest bugs and other creepy creatures / by M.L. Roberts.
    p.   cm.
    Includes index.
    ISBN 0-8167-3536-0 (lib.) ISBN 0-8167-3537-9 (pbk.)
    1. Insects—Juvenile literature. 2. Spiders—Juvenile literature.
    [1. Insects.] I. Title.
    QL467.2.R631995
    595.7—dc20   94-18027

Printed in the United States of America.

10 9 8 7 6 5 4 3 2 1

Photo credits:

All photos courtesy of Tom Stack & Associates. Photos on pages 3, 11, 17, 19, and 27 © by David M. Dennis; page 5 © by Robert C. Simpson; pages 7 and 21 © by Denise Tackett; page 9 © by Cristopher Crowley; page 13 © by John Shaw; pages 15, 25, and 31 © by Rod Planck; page 23 © by Kerry T. Givens; page 29 © by George D. Dodge.

Cover photo of peanut-head bug © by Chip Isenhart, courtesy of Tom Stack & Associates.

The peanut-head bug

The bug on the cover belongs to a family of insects often called *lantern flies*. That's because people once mistakenly believed that the peanut-shaped, hollow part of their bodies gave off light! Some lantern flies secrete a white wax that may stream behind them when the insects fly. They are often brilliantly colored, with a wingspread of up to 6 inches (15 cm).